Though Unmanifest God Is Most Manifest

ISBN : 1430418621

A. S. Raleigh

Kessinger Publishing's Rare Reprints

Thousands of Scarce and Hard-to-Find Books on These and other Subjects!

- Americana
- Ancient Mysteries
- Animals
- Anthropology
- Architecture
- Arts
- Astrology
- Bibliographies
- Biographies & Memoirs
- Body, Mind & Spirit
- Business & Investing
- Children & Young Adult
- Collectibles
- Comparative Religions
- Crafts & Hobbies
- Earth Sciences
- Education
- Ephemera
- Fiction
- Folklore
- Geography
- Health & Diet
- History
- Hobbies & Leisure
- Humor
- Illustrated Books
- Language & Culture
- Law
- Life Sciences

- Literature
- Medicine & Pharmacy
- Metaphysical
- Music
- Mystery & Crime
- Mythology
- Natural History
- Outdoor & Nature
- Philosophy
- Poetry
- Political Science
- Science
- Psychiatry & Psychology
- Reference
- Religion & Spiritualism
- Rhetoric
- Sacred Books
- Science Fiction
- Science & Technology
- Self-Help
- Social Sciences
- Symbolism
- Theatre & Drama
- Theology
- Travel & Explorations
- War & Military
- Women
- Yoga
- *Plus Much More!*

**We kindly invite you to view our catalog list at:
http://www.kessinger.net**

PHILOSOPHIA HERMETICA

Though Unmanifest God Is Most Manifest.

(Text: G. R. S. Mead. Thrice Greatest Hermes; Corpus Hermeticum (VI); G. Parthey, Hermetis Trismegisti, 41-48; Patrizzi, Nova de Universis Philosophia, 12b-13b.)

1. I will recount to thee this sermon *(logos)* too, O Tat, that thou mayest cease to be without the mysteries of the God beyond all name. And mark thou well how That which to the many seems unmanifest, will grow most manifest for thee.

Now, were It manifest, It would not *be.* For all that is made manifest is subject to *becoming,* for it hath been *made* manifest. But the Unmanifest forever *is,* for It doth not desire to be made manifest. It ever is, and maketh manifest all other things.

Being Himself unmanifest, as ever being and ever making-manifest, Himself is not made manifest. God is not made Himself; by thinking-manifest, He thinketh all things manifest.

Now "thinking-manifest" deals with things made alone, for thinking-manifest is nothing else than making.

2. He, then, alone who is not made, 'tis clear, is both beyond all power of thinking-manifest, and is unmanifest.

And as He thinketh all things manifest, He manifests through all things and in all, and most of all in whatsoever things He wills to manifest.

7

Do thou, then, Tat, my son, pray first unto our Lord and Father, the One-and-Only One, from whom the One doth come, to show His mercy unto thee, in order that thou mayest have the power to catch a thought of this so mighty God, one single beam of Him to shine into thy thinking. For thought alone "sees" the Unmanifest, in that it is itself unmanifest.

If, then, thou hast the power, He will, Tat, manifest to thy mind's eyes. The Lord begrudges not Himself to anything, but manifests Himself through the whole world.

Thou hast the power of taking thought, of seeing it and grasping it in thy own "hands," and gazing face to face upon God's Image. But if what is within thee even is unmanifest to thee, how, then, shall He Himself who is within thy self be manifest for thee by means of [outer] eyes?

3. But if thou wouldst "see" Him, bethink thee of the sun, bethink thee of moon's course, bethink thee of the order of the stars. Who is the One who watcheth o'er that order? For every order hath its boundaries marked out by place and number.

The sun's the greatest god of gods in heaven; to whom all the heavenly gods give place as unto king and master. And he, this so-great one, he greater than the earth and sea, endures to have above him circling smaller stars than him. Out of respect to Whom, or out of fear of Whom, my son, [doth he do this]?

Nor like nor equal is the course each of these stars describes in heaven. Who [then] is He who marketh out the manner of their course and its extent?

4. The Bear up there that turneth round

itself, and carries round the whole cosmos
with it—Who is the owner of this instru-
ment? Who He who hath set round the sea
its bounds? Who He who hath set on its
seat the earth?

For, Tat, there *is* someone who is the
Maker and the Lord of all these things. It
could not be that number, place and measure
could be kept without someone to make them.
No order whatsoever could be made by that
which lacketh place and lacketh measure;
nay; even this is not without a Lord, my son.
For if the orderless lacks something, in that
it is not lord of order's path, it also is beneath
a lord—the one who hath not yet ordained it
order.

5. Would it were possible for thee to get
thee wings, and soar into the air, and, poised
midway 'tween earth and heaven, behold the
earth's solidity, the sea's fluidity (the flowing
of its streams), the spaciousness of air, fire's
swiftness, [and] the coursing of the stars, the
swiftness of heaven's circuit round them
[all]!

Most blessed sight were it, my son, to see
all these beneath one sway—the motionless in
motion, and the unmanifest made manifest;
whereby is made this order of the cosmos and
the cosmos which we see of order.

6. If thou would'st see Him too through
things that suffer death, both on the earth
and in the deep, think of a man's being fash-
ioned in the womb, my son, and strictly scru-
tinize the art of Him who fashions him, and
learn who fashioneth this fair and godly
image of the Man.

Who [then] is He who traceth out the circles of the eyes; who He who boreth out the nostrils and the ears; who He who openeth [the portal of] the mouth; who He who doth stretch out and tie the nerves; who He who channels out the veins; who He who hardeneth the bones; who He who covereth the flesh with skin; who He who separates the fingers and the joints; who He who widens out a treading for the feet; who He who diggeth out the ducts; who He who spreadeth out the spleen; who He who shapeth heart like to a pyramid; who He who setteth ribs together; who He who wideneth the liver out; who He who maketh lungs like to a sponge; who He who maketh belly stretch so much; who He who doth make prominent the parts most honorable, so that they may be seen, while hiding out of sight those of least honor?

7. Behold how many arts [employed] on one material, how many labors on one single sketch; and all exceeding fair, and all in perfect measure, yet all diversified! Who made them all? what mother, or what sire, save God alone, unmanifest, who hath made all things by His Will?

8. And no one saith a statue or a picture comes to be without a sculptor or [without] a painter; doth [then] such workmanship as this exist without a Worker? What depth of blindness, what deep impiety, what depth of ignorance! See, then, thou ne'er, son Tat, deprivest works of Worker!

Nay, rather is He greater than all names, so great is He, the Father of them all. For verily He is the Only One; and this His work, to be a father.

9. So, if thou forcest me somewhat too bold,

to speak, His being is conceiving of all things and making [them].

And as without its maker it is impossible that anything should be, so ever is He not unless He ever makes all things, in heaven, in air, in earth, in deep, in all of cosmos, in every part that is and that is not of everything. For there is naught in all the world that is not He.

He is Himself, both things that are and things that are not. The things that are He hath made manifest, He keepeth things that are not in Himself.

He is the God beyond all name; He the unmanifest, He the most manifest; He whom the mind [alone] can contemplate, He visible unto the eyes [as well]; He is the one of no body, the one of many bodies, nay, rather He of every body.

Naught is there which He is not. For all are He and He is all. And for this cause hath He all names, in that they are one Father's. And for this cause hath He Himself no name, in that He's Father of [them] all.

Who, then, may sing Thee praise of Thee, or [praise] to Thee?

Whither, again, am I to turn my eyes to sing Thy praise; above, below, within, without?

There is no way, no place [is there] about Thee, nor any other thing of things that are.

All [are] in Thee; all [are] from Thee; O Thou who givest all takest naught, for Thou hast all and naught is there Thou hast not.

11. And *when*, O Father, shall I hymn Thee? For none can seize Thy hour or time.

For what, again, shall I sing hymn? For things that Thou hast made, or things Thou hast not? For things Thou hast made manifest, or things Thou hast concealed?

How, further, shall I hymn Thee? As being of myself? As having something of mine own? As being other?

For that Thou art whatever I may be; Thou art whatever I may do; Thou art whatever I may speak.

For Thou art all, and there is nothing else which Thou art not. Thou art all that which doth exist, and Thou art what doth not exist, —Mind when Thou thinkest, and Father when Thou makest, and God when Thou dost energize, and Good and Maker of all things.

(For that the subtler part of matter is the air, of air the soul, of soul the mind, and of mind God.)